JONI'S STORY

Discovering Hope That Endures

Joni's Story: Discovering Hope That Endures

Copyright © 2022 Joni & Friends. All rights reserved.

Print ISBN: 978-1-946237-52-1

Kindle ISBN: 978-1-946237-54-5

EPUB ISBN: 978-1-946237-53-8

Unless otherwise indicated, all Scripture quotations are taken from the *Holy Bible*, New Living Translation, copyright © 1996, 2004, 2015 by Tyndale House Foundation. Used by permission of Tyndale House Publishers, Inc., Carol Stream, Illinois 60188. All rights reserved.

Scriptures marked ESV are taken from The ESV® Bible (The Holy Bible, English Standard Version®). ESV® Text Edition: 2016. Copyright © 2001 by Crossway, a publishing ministry of Good News Publishers. The ESV® text has been reproduced in cooperation with and by permission of Good News Publishers. Unauthorized reproduction of this publication is prohibited.
All rights reserved.

Scriptures marked NIV are taken from THE HOLY BIBLE, NEW INTERNATIONAL VERSION®, NIV® Copyright © 1973, 1978, 1984, 2011 by Biblica, Inc.® Used by permission. All rights reserved worldwide.

JONI'S STORY

Discovering Hope That Endures

JONI EARECKSON TADA

NO GOING BACK

Though he brings grief, he also shows compassion because of the greatness of his unfailing love. For he does not enjoy hurting people or causing them sorrow.
—Lamentations 3:32-33

The wail of the siren made it hard for me to think. I kept trying to make sense of my limp arms and legs, and the weird electrical jolt I'd felt when my head hit the sand after my dive into the bay. Why hadn't I been able to swim back to the surface? Why couldn't I feel my arms as my sister Kathy struggled to pull me out of the water? And why weren't the paramedics talking to me as the ambulance I was in raced through the city streets?

"Hey, I'm sure I'll be fine in a minute or two. Just give me a chance to clear my head. There's no reason to keep the lights and siren on. I'm just a little stunned. There's no reason to disrupt everyone else's quiet summer day."

But the emergency medical team continued to avoid my eyes. And when I got to the hospital, the medical staff there didn't make eye contact either. It was worse now, though, because so much didn't make sense. One nurse pulled out hair trimmers and by the time I could understand why, my protests were drowned out by the buzz as my blonde hair fell in uneven clumps onto the floor. Then another nurse approached with a pair of sheers, and I watched in horror as she snipped through my favorite new bathing suit.

"Just wait a minute!" I wanted to scream. "I'm okay. I'm just a little stunned! Give me a minute, and I'll be happy to change out of it."

No one gave me a minute. They all worked quickly and efficiently, only speaking with each other.

Finally, the doctor walked in. At last, someone was talking to me. He pulled out a pin and did something out of my line of sight, asking me if I could feel it.

"No," I said.

He slowly worked his way closer to my head, and I could see he was using the pin to poke my hands then my shoulders.

There! I felt a prick.

He nodded his head. Minutes later another doctor joined him. They spoke in hushed tones, something about a severed cervical column. I didn't understand, and neither doctor stopped to explain.

What was going on?!

I wished for my father, the most capable man I knew. He would help straighten things out. He could fix just about anything he set his mind to. Certainly he could straighten out this little mess I'd somehow stumbled into.

I wished for my mother, full of energy and perceptive insight. She'd stop those doctors and make them talk straight to me.

Or even my sister Kathy. She certainly should be here somewhere. She was the one who had helped me out of the water after that foolish dive I'd attempted. Why had no one brought her in to see me?

What was happening? Did anyone care?

I felt so alone.

GOD'S GREAT COMPASSION

For the grace of God has been revealed, bringing salvation to all people....We should live in this evil world with wisdom, righteousness, and devotion to God, while we look forward with hope to that wonderful day when the glory of our great God and Savior, Jesus Christ, will be revealed. He gave his life to free us from every kind of sin, to cleanse us, and to make us his very own people, totally committed to doing good deeds.
—Titus 2:11–14

Those dark days in the hospital after breaking my neck brought me face-to-face with suffering and hardship for the first time in my life. I'd grown up in a loving family. My athletic mother was always quick to lend a helping hand to anyone who had need of it. My father was a hard worker, strong and talented. I, as the youngest of four sisters, was named after him. Around our relatives, he was often called "Big Johnny," and I was "Little Johnny."

My family lived an active life. We loved almost any opportunity to get outdoors. Even though I was the youngest, I was determined to keep up. Camping, hiking, horses, sports—I wanted to do it all.

What's more, the people in our little corner of the world respected my family. We worshiped at a small church nearby, and I enjoyed the company of the popular kids at school. My parents knew Jesus and worked hard to instill in me gospel truths, but as a teenager, I made choices I'm not proud of. Disobedience ruled my life.

Never did I feel this more keenly than shortly after my fourteenth birthday. I tagged along with kids from the popular crowd to a Christian camp for young people. One night, after the lesson, everyone stood to sing an old hymn I had known for a long time, "And Can It Be." When we reached the fourth verse, the truth of the words written long ago by Charles Wesley struck me in a way it never had before. Half in song, half in prayer, I confessed the truths:

Long my imprisoned spirit lay
Fast bound in sin and nature's night.

Oh, Jesus, I prayed, *I am completely bound by my sin. I am imprisoned by it. I don't know exactly what I need to do, but my life isn't working. I feel so lost in the dark.*

I woke, the dungeon flamed with light;
My chains fell off, my heart was free,
I rose, went forth, and followed Thee.

I understand now. I can see I've been in a dungeon of my own making. I want your freedom, Jesus. Help me to say no to sin and follow you. I want to be out of this dungeon. I want my chains of sin to fall off. I do want to follow you.

Amazing love! How can it be
That Thou, my God, should die for me?

That was the start of a great longing for God in my heart. And yet, while I meant that prayer, as the months and years slipped by, the way I lived Monday through Saturday grew less and less consistent with what I said I believed on Sunday. It seemed I just couldn't stop sinning, no matter what I committed in my heart. It saddened me, but I seemed powerless. My final year of high school, as I looked toward graduation and college, the contradiction between what I said and what I did scared me, and so I prayed, "God, please do something."

And then a few months later, there I was lying on a hospital gurney, unable to move my arms and legs. Is this how God answers prayer? Did he see my desperate prayer at the disgust of my sin as a license to "do his worst"?

No. God saw my plea as my heart's true cry: I longed to worship him not just with the words of my mouth, but with my whole being. And since that is God's true desire for me too, he permitted events that would bring this to pass.

HOPE DEFERRED

My suffering was good for me, for it taught me to pay attention to your decrees. —Psalm 119:71

I wasn't thinking all this that first afternoon, scared beyond words as the doctors and nurses talked over me like I wasn't there. It wasn't on my mind as one nurse buzzed my hair with electric clippers, preparing me for a surgery to stabilize my neck using great big bolts. Nor was I thinking about it during the long, difficult months of rehabilitation that followed.

During that time, I couldn't accept I would never walk again. I just knew God would heal my spinal cord, and since I was convinced it was going to happen, I didn't see much point in the types of therapy aimed at helping me learn how to "make do" with the little shoulder movement I had. I wanted the kind of therapy that would get me walking again! And because that is where all my hope lay, I didn't see much point in prayer, except to ask God to heal me.

Proverbs 13:12 says, "Hope deferred makes the heart sick." And oh, my heart was sick. As the months and years passed, and I still did not regain the use of my hands and legs, I sank into a dark depression. I assumed God was not answering my prayers for healing, that there must be something wrong with me—a lack of faith or some unconfessed sin—that kept God from making my body whole again. I confessed every sin I could think of and even made a few up to confess just in case.

After I was discharged from the hospital, I spent days stubbornly tucked away in a darkened bedroom. I felt there was no life beyond my door. Even when I did participate in my family's comings and goings, pressure sores or a bout with the flu put me back in that spot of depression and wondering when death would come.

But one day, desperate and weary from my own hopelessness, I cried out: "God, if I can't die, please show me how to live!"

GOD ANSWERS PRAYER

Your promise revives me; it comforts me in all my troubles.
—Psalm 119:50

God answered that prayer through Christian friends who took the time to show me what the Bible says about suffering. I vaguely understood the truth that God's Word was my only source of hope and help, but I had no idea where to begin. Who was there to guide me? Who would sit next to me in my wheelchair, open a Bible, and work to find answers to my hard questions about depression, healing, and what it means to say God is in control?

I had so many questions for God, and in his goodness, he sent an unlikely person to help me find answers. God sent a kid a few years younger than me. His name was Steve.

Even as a teenager, Steve understood the Bible held the answers to my questions, and he was committed to helping me find them. One day, as I struggled to understand why God didn't stop me from breaking my neck, Steve told me, "Joni, God permits what he hates to accomplish what he loves."

I knew then that if God had some good purpose in mind for me when my neck snapped underwater, then I wanted to search out that purpose. I didn't want to "waste" my suffering!

GOD AT WORK IN MY DISABILITY

I have told you these things so that you will be filled with my joy. Yes, your joy will overflow! —John 15:11

The more I began to trust God with my life of paralysis, the more contentment I experienced. With contentment, I found new pleasure in creating art. While I was in the hospital, an occupational therapist had challenged me to try drawing by placing a pencil between my teeth. At first, I thought it was foolish for me to try, but over time, I realized it was a way to show the joy I had found in Jesus Christ. Every time I would sign my name to another piece of art, I would add "PTL," which stands for "Praise the Lord," because I wanted people to worship God whenever they saw my name.

No one was more surprised than me to discover I had an ever-widening audience for the work of God in my life. It was amazing that God could use me, a girl with a broken neck, to encourage people from God's Word. But I was reminded of Isaiah 50:4, which says, "The Sovereign LORD has given me his words of wisdom, so that I know how to comfort the weary." I began sharing the story of God's goodness to me with small group gatherings near my home. Over time, I traveled further and further to tell what I had learned about God's grace from my wheelchair.

Soon my artwork caught the attention of a local television station. Their reporting led to an interview on network TV. There, on a national broadcast, I shared the reason for my joyful spirit: "It's all because of Jesus Christ, my Savior. I'd be hopeless without him!"

My artwork and my wheelchair gave me a platform from which I could speak boldly about God's goodness and love. When I realized this, I committed to being God's best audio-visual aid to the world, demonstrating how his grace shows up best in weakness. I wanted to bring glory to God by giving evidence of how his amazing grace sustained me through every weakness I encountered.

SHARING HOPE

You intended to harm me, but God intended it all for good. He brought me to this position so I could save the lives of many people. —Genesis 50:20

I will never forget the day that my desire to display God's amazing grace expanded beyond anything I'd felt before. One day, when I was back at the rehabilitation center for a medical check-up, I encountered a paraplegic sitting by the elevator in his wheelchair. I smiled and introduced myself, asking, "What's your name?" He only shrugged his shoulders in reply. I had never seen such hopelessness and despair. It was as though he were trying to disappear.

That man's response stunned me to my core. I had been in a similar position only a few years earlier. So many times I sat by that very elevator, watching people walk by, a sour expression on my face. Yet now, I wasn't that person anymore. I had found hope.

Right then and there, I saw the crystal-clear difference Jesus Christ can make in the life of someone with a disability. I wondered if perhaps God intended to use my paralysis to help other people like this man—other people like me—find hope in Jesus Christ. When I left that rehab center, I resolved to do everything I could to submit my life to God's plan so he might use my suffering to save the lives of many people.

BUSY IN MINISTRY

*I am the L*ORD*, the God of all the peoples of the world. Is anything too hard for me? —Jeremiah 32:27*

The years that followed were filled with all manner of things I could not have imagined during those long, dark nights in the hospital. A publisher, amazed at the joy I displayed during my interview on national television, invited me to write a book. After the book released, I was asked to star in a movie based on the book! I began getting hundreds of letters. Each letter contained so many questions, many of them from people with disabilities like me. I knew that the only way I could really help each person—even those suffering in ways I could only imagine—was to share the truths I discovered from God's Word. I saw 2 Corinthians 1:4 at work, "He comforts us in all our troubles so that we can comfort others. When they are troubled, we will be able to give them the same comfort God has given us."

With the needs of so many people in mind, I began the ministry of Joni and Friends to bring God's hope to hurting people. Soon the words of Jesus in Luke 14 took on new meaning in my life as I read the Lord's command to "invite the poor, the crippled, the blind, and the lame....so that the house will be full" (vv. 21, 23). I knew God wanted people with disabilities to enjoy his eternal celebration in heaven, and I wanted to take part in his plan to make that happen. The more I studied, the more I understood God's heart on the matter: it's not merely good to include people with disabilities; it's necessary! First Corinthians 12:20–22 says, "Yes, there are many parts, but only one body. The eye can never say to the hand, 'I don't need you.' The head can't say to the feet, 'I don't need you.' In fact, some parts of the body that seem weakest and least important are actually the most necessary."

Like the name *Joni and Friends* suggests, I relied on many friends to be my hands and feet as I started this new ministry. I had moved far away from family to begin Joni and Friends, so I needed friends to help me do just about everything! It was at the home of one of these friends where I met a very special someone named Ken Tada. Ken soon became a dear friend, and not long after that, he asked me to marry him. Even though we weren't sure how we'd make marriage work, we committed to honoring God together with our lives, and God blessed us in that commitment.

In this season, it was easy to see the good things God was doing because of my broken neck. So many people were hearing about God's love for the first time. The ministry of Joni and Friends was expanding around the world, equipping churches and delivering the good news of Jesus to people with disabilities. Ken and I were busy meeting needs in our community and internationally. I began to think I was seeing all that God had wanted when he permitted my accident. What he was accomplishing was certainly wonderful and good!

I thought I had God's good plan more or less figured out during those busy years of ministry until I encountered an enormous speed bump: chronic pain.

LEANING HARD ON GOD

Each time he said, "My grace is all you need. My power works best in weakness." So now I am glad to boast about my weaknesses, so that the power of Christ can work through me.
—2 Corinthians 12:9

The airplane I was sitting in began to descend as it approached the airport. I was so relieved to be nearly on the ground. I wanted so badly to get out of my narrow seat and get home. Under any conditions, this would have been a long flight—I was wrapping up an extended international ministry trip—but these weren't just any conditions. The pain between my shoulders was so intense that it felt as though a knife were twisting back and forth in my back. I'd dealt with pain before, but nothing like this. Nothing that made me feel so desperate for relief.

I'd been working long hours, eager to see all God was doing through Joni and Friends around the world. *Surely, with some rest and a visit or two to the doctor, I'll be back to my usual health and energy*, I thought. After all, God would certainly be able to do more ministry work through me if I were feeling well, rather than distracted and derailed by pain.

God had other plans.

Test by test, my doctors and I ruled out potential sources of the pain. With no answer to the cause of the problem, treatment seemed impossible, and relief out of reach. The future seemed bleak. How could I continue living the rest of my life with such biting pain? How could I continue leading a ministry that was growing larger by the day? How could I do all that I longed to do? And what could I do about the depression that lurked in the corners of my day, the dark feelings that waited to consume me whenever the pain stole my breath away?

Finally, it came: the only reasonable answer for the pain were the years of quadriplegia. I had been sitting in a wheelchair day in and day out, and my pain was simply a result of weakened muscles and scoliosis in my spine. In short, the pain was here to stay.

I could not stand to let the feelings of depression pull me down like they had when I first became paralyzed. I'd learned that God's grace had no limit, and so I leaned all the harder on his promises. And the harder I leaned on God, the stronger I discovered him to be. God had more to teach me, and it was in the school of pain.

In this new suffering, I also discovered a new ministry. When I began to speak of the pain that chased sleep away and made concentrating during the day nearly impossible, I heard from so many individuals who knew the same difficult story of chronic pain. As I became friends with people whose pain had kept them in bed for years, unable to touch or be touched, I discovered a fellowship of suffering. Each of us found new purpose in encouraging and reminding each other of God's goodness in the dark of a night filled with pain.

JESUS IN MY SUFFERING

So whether you eat or drink, or whatever you do, do it all for the glory of God. – 1 Corinthians 10:31

Because so much of my attention was consumed by my pain, when I discovered I had breast cancer, it was already stage 3. Everything in my life came to a standstill. In the same way that my chronic pain had been unknown territory because of limited information about decades-long quadriplegia, my doctors weren't sure how my weakened muscles would withstand a difficult treatment regimen. And because chemotherapy lowered my resistance to germs, I was encouraged to stay at home.

I wasn't certain how to fill the long days, but then Ephesians 5:10 told me what to do: "Find out what pleases the Lord" (NIV) and do it. I knew prayer pleased God, and so after someone helped me eat breakfast, I would spend extra time in prayer, covering my concerns both big and small. Then I would ask, "What will please you now, Lord?"

Some days I knew the most important way to please God was to eat sixty-five grams of protein before lunch. Other times it was to back away from my computer to enjoy the hummingbirds at the bird feeder. During this season, I learned to depend constantly on God and to see how everything I did—eating, drinking, praying, singing—could be done for his glory.

When I first received my cancer diagnosis, I thought maybe it was God's way of telling me my work on earth was finally done. I would face this one more challenge, and then I could leave suffering behind. Yet the more I prayed, I realized this cancer wasn't the end. Instead, it was another way that God was permitting what he hated to accomplish what he loved.

Yes, it was still a hard path, but it was leading me toward a glorious eternity, just as 2 Corinthians 4:16–18 says, "Though our bodies are dying, our spirits are being renewed every day. For our present troubles are small and won't last very long. Yet they produce for us a glory that vastly outweighs them and will last forever! So we don't look at the troubles we can see now; rather, we fix our gaze on things that cannot be seen. For the things we see now will soon be gone, but the things we cannot see will last forever."

I thought about this truth in a whole new way one day when Ken was driving me home from a session of chemotherapy. We were sobered by the hard things we were experiencing and the thought that sufferings in this life are "splash-overs of hell,"—awful, gut-wrenching reminders of the horrors Jesus Christ rescues us from. As Ken pulled into our driveway, we then wondered, *What are splash-overs of heaven? Are they easy, bright times when everything's going right*?

After a long silence, Ken looked at me and with tears in his eyes and whispered, "No, Joni. It's when we see Jesus in our splash-over of hell."

My appreciation for how God rescued me through the death and resurrection of Jesus Christ became more complete as I experienced his comfort and nearness in the darkness of my battle with cancer.

JOY IN GOD'S PRESENCE

You will show me the way of life, granting me the joy of your presence and the pleasures of living with you forever.
—Psalm 16:11

We celebrated big when I received the "all clear" after the rigorous cancer treatment. The celebration was all the bigger when we reflected on how God had once again used my suffering to show me more of his goodness and had also allowed me to share what I was learning with others fighting cancer. Had I never battled stage 3 breast cancer, I never would have had the opportunity to share the hope I had found in Jesus with thousands of women and their families.

This is the only reason I can offer for why I received unexpected news eight years later: my cancer was back. When my oncologist shared the diagnosis, I relaxed and smiled, knowing that my sovereign God loves me dearly and holds me tightly in his hands. After all, what good is it if we only trust the Lord when we understand his reasons?

Because this cancer was a reoccurrence of the original cancer, my doctors recommended a very aggressive treatment plan. It could have been so easy to let myself be overwhelmed, but I kept thinking back to the way God had cared for me through so many other challenges. All around my bedroom, I placed reminders of God's faithfulness—how he had rescued me from becoming overwhelmed and hopeless in the past. With those reminders in view, it was easier to trust he would be faithful to do the same in this new trial.

JESUS CAN BE TRUSTED

My purpose is to give them a rich and satisfying life. —John 10:10

You might think that so many physical problems would cause me to doubt God's trustworthiness. Instead, I have seen each new challenge as a way to dig deeper into God's Word, to lean harder into the truths I know about God, and to draw closer to Jesus Christ, my Savior. I know that if cancer grows a third time, or if my chronic pain continues to advance, or if there is some other trial around the next corner—I know, and have every confidence, that God will demonstrate his faithfulness to me again by giving me courage, perseverance, and a bright new capacity to trust him in a deeper way.

I don't mean to say that it is all easy. Every single year of my quadriplegia has been lived one day at a time, sometimes so moment-by-moment that I barely thought I could endure one moment more. But God has seen me through every minute, giving me a greater experience of his peace, joy, and contentment. Because of this, I don't focus on my visible wheelchair, arm braces, and other symbols of my earthly weaknesses. Instead, I focus on unseen things like the spirit of gratitude God has cultivated within me, the patience I've honed, and my longing for heaven, which has eclipsed the sorrows of earth.

And I know now what it is God loves so much that he permitted my broken neck, the cancer, the chronic pain, and every other trial I've endured. It's just like Colossians 1:27 says, "the riches and glory of Christ are for you....Christ lives in you. This gives you assurance of sharing his glory." This is what God loves: Christ in me, the hope of glory. To have Christ in me is to be more like Christ, to replace the old, self-absorbed Joni with one who thanks God for what he has taught me in the school of suffering so that I might value him even more.

For sure, I can hardly wait for that day when I receive complete healing in heaven! With my new, glorified legs, I will run to Jesus and drop to my knees before him, my King. With healed arms, I will lift my hands in praise and embrace the nail-pierced hands of Jesus my Savior. But most of all, I look forward to worshiping God with a new heart—a heart free of sin, sorrow, and selfishness.

A FINAL WORD

God blesses those who patiently endure testing and temptation. Afterward they will receive the crown of life that God promises to those who love him. —James 1:12

Oh, friend, I don't know what your life looks like or why you've chosen to read my story. But I pray that as you think about my life, you'll be challenged to pray and ask God what he wants for you.

And if you aren't quite sure what your next step might be, let me suggest that you start with reading God's Word, the Bible. Even though God has used my story to introduce many to his love and goodness, I know my life isn't enough to transform hearts. Only God can do that—and he does it as his Spirit reveals the truth of his Word to your heart and mind. That's why I've included so many verses from the Bible in telling my story. They have been signposts throughout my life, and they can be for you too.

NEXT STEPS

A NEW CREATION

In the beginning, God created a good and beautiful world with no grief or sorrow, no death or disease. He formed everything we can see and everything we can't see—from mollusks to mathematics and geraniums to giraffes—and it was all very good. Then he made the first human beings to live with him and be part of his family.

The struggles and challenges we experience today—whether physical, emotional, social, or intellectual—are foreign to God's original design for creation. We live in the aftermath of history's greatest tragedy, and the suffering we encounter is one of the aftershocks.

The Bible tells us Adam and Eve chose to believe a lie of Satan; they trusted the serpent instead of the One who made them, cared for them, and loved them beyond measure. And so, with a bite of forbidden fruit, the world became infected with an insidious disease. The goodness of creation, while not lost, was bent and twisted out of shape. Sin took hold of our first parents; shame washed over them, and death followed them the rest of their days. This broken and jagged legacy has been passed down ever since. On our own we cannot escape it.

Thank God we are not on our own!

God loves humanity. He sent his one and only Son, Jesus, to earth to show us what God's heart is like. Then Jesus died. He shed his blood on a Roman cross, taking our place. He paid the price for our sins and made a way for us to come back home to the Father. But his death was not the end of the story. On the third day, he rose to new life. He became the firstborn of a new creation, one that restores the goodness, beauty, and truth we lost so long ago.

I heard a loud shout from the throne, saying, "Look, God's home is now among his people! He will live with them, and they will be his people. God himself will be with them. He will wipe every tear from their eyes, and there will be no more death or sorrow or crying or pain. All these things are gone forever." (*Revelation 21:3–4*)

This is the *gospel*—the "good news" of Jesus Christ. Because of Jesus' death and resurrection, we can have peace with God and be welcomed into his family as a son or daughter of the King. When we do, he will send his Holy Spirit to live inside of us so that we will never again be separated from his love. The Spirit also helps us to become more like Jesus as we walk with him each day. His presence in our lives is our assurance that all of God's promises are true!

This incredible gift of God can't be bought with money or good works. It isn't reserved for those with power or certain talents either. In fact, Jesus has a special place in his heart for the meek, the humble, and the poor. All that is required to become a follower of Jesus and a child of God is to believe.

That's right—Jesus simply asks us to believe he is the Son of God and to put our full trust in him as our Savior and Lord. When we give ourselves to him as he gave himself for us, we are saved. He takes our sins and shame, and exchanges them for new life and new purpose.

If you've never prayed to become a follower of Jesus Christ, you can do so today! Here is a suggested prayer, but feel free to use your own words. There is no secret formula, no special phrases required. God looks at your heart!

Heavenly Father,
I know that I am a sinner. I have broken Your commandments, and my life has not honored You

the way it should. Thank You for sending Your Son, Jesus, to die for my sins. Here and now, I put my faith and trust in him and him alone for my salvation. Help me to follow him closely every day of my life. Thank You for the gift of Your Spirit and the promise of a new creation. Thank You for welcoming me into Your family. I love You. Amen.

If you've prayed to receive Jesus as your Lord and Savior, welcome to the family! The Bible tells us that "anyone who belongs to Christ has become a new person. The old life is gone; a new life has begun!" (2 Corinthians 5:17).

You may be thinking, *What does this new life look like? What do I do now?* You've become a Christian by faith, and so you are now called to live this new life by faith. There will be difficulties that come your way, but Jesus gives us this promise: "Here on earth you will have many trials and sorrows. But take heart, because I have overcome the world" (John 16:33). Just stick closely to Jesus, and he will guide you.

With that in mind, there are some things every new believer should know....

NOW THAT YOU BELIEVE

The Bible

There are lots and lots of books in the world, but the Bible is different from all of them. It is a gift beyond measure, for it contains the very words of God. Without God choosing to reveal himself to humanity, we would be helplessly lost and without hope. Thankfully, in his goodness, God saw fit to bend low from the heavens and speak to people who were lost and far away from him.

The Bible is a collection of inspired writings that carry the weight and authority of God himself. The books of the Bible were penned by human beings but "breathed out by God" (2 Timothy 3:16 ESV). That means that for every passage of the Bible, there are at least two authors—one human and one divine.

The human author wrote from a specific place and time, with a worldview shaped by his surroundings. That's why sometimes certain Bible passages or customs mentioned can sound strange to us. It's also why it's important to try and understand what a verse meant to its original audience before applying it to our lives today.

The human authors of Scripture "spoke from God as they were carried along by the Holy Spirit" (2 Peter 1:21 ESV). From Genesis to Revelation, the Spirit of God directed and inspired every word. So, as we study the Bible, we shouldn't be surprised to find there are connections that transcend books, genres, and even the original ancient languages. Though the Bible is a library of sixty-six individual volumes, it's still one coherent and beautiful book.

As believers, we are invited and called to read and study God's Word, not simply to increase our understanding of God, ourselves, and this world, but also to draw near to God's heart—to fall more deeply in love with him as we discover his holiness, goodness, and mercy. The Bible also helps us to learn our roles in the grand story of redemption. In this book, we've included a few suggested Bible reading plans to get you started. Before you dive in, however, here are a few things to keep in mind:

- Reading your Bible might seem like a solo activity—just you and the Word of God—but the Holy Spirit,

who lives inside of you, promises to illuminate the Scriptures as you read in faith (Ephesians 1:17–18). Pray (we'll get to prayer in a moment) and ask the Lord for understanding and wisdom. Jesus himself promised, "When the Spirit of truth comes, he will guide you into all truth" (John 16:13). Trust him to do so.
- As we've already mentioned, the Bible was written by human authors who lived a long time ago in cultures different from our own. So, while the Bible is absolutely *for you*, it wasn't written *to you*. Therefore, do your best to understand the original context before applying what you read to your life today. When you come across something you don't understand, it's a good idea to seek the wisdom of a more mature Christian or your pastor.
- While many people make it their goal to read through the Bible in a year, there is no finish line. Bible study should be a lifelong joy that is never complete. The Bible is good food for the soul; it's important to partake every day.

Prayer

When you stop to think that God created billions of galaxies and trillions of stars—and knows each one by name—it's an awesome thing to know we can talk to him directly. More than that, he invites us to bring our questions, our heartaches, and our struggles with us. In short, prayer is talking to God. We are God's children, and prayer is our lifeline to the Father. As it is with any relationship, it's important to spend time together. Prayer is one of the ways we do that.

When Jesus walked the earth, he instructed his disciples to pray and gave them this model prayer:

Our Father in heaven,
 may your name be kept holy.
May your Kingdom come soon.
May your will be done on earth,
 as it is in heaven.
Give us today the food we need,
and forgive us our sins,
 as we have forgiven those who sin against us.
And don't let us yield to temptation,
 but rescue us from the evil one.
    (Matthew 6:9–13)

Scripture itself is a wonderful resource when we can't find the words to match the thoughts and emotions swirling in our hearts. (The book of Psalms is an excellent place to find words to express your feelings.) And while it's certainly fine to pray these words given to us by Jesus, prayer cannot remain limited to repeated words and phrases. Even so, the Lord's prayer offers us an approach to prayer that every follower of Jesus can emulate.

- *Our Father in heaven, may your name be kept holy.* The prayer starts with **praise and worship**. By addressing God as "Father" and acknowledging his holiness, we honor him and set our hearts in the right place to enter into his presence.
- *May your Kingdom come soon. May your will be done on earth, as it is in heaven.* Next, there is the recognition that God is the true King over the entire universe. His will is what matters, not our own. In this we **offer submission of our wants, desires, and even our needs to him**.

- *Give us today the food we need*, ... Then, we **ask him to supply our needs**, acknowledging that he is the God who provides and the source of every good thing.
- *.... and forgive us our sins*, ... We confess our sins and ask for forgiveness. When we know of specific transgressions and failings, we ought to come clean before God. We cannot hide from him anyway, and he invites us to bring our sins to him in order to be cleansed (see 1 John 1:9).
- *.... as we have forgiven those who sin against us.* Of course, sins don't only flow in one direction. There are people who sin against us. When we pray, it's an opportunity to **ask for the Lord's help in cultivating forgiveness**. It's been said that holding a grudge is like drinking poison and hoping the other person gets sick. Forgiveness, on the other hand, sets us free.
- *And don't let us yield to temptation, but rescue us from the evil one.* Finally, **prayer arms us for spiritual warfare**. God never tempts anyone (James 1:13–14), but we fall into temptation more easily when we don't ask God for his help. "The evil one" refers to Satan, the enemy of God and his people. Thankfully, God does not leave us defenseless against his attacks. In prayer, we ask God to give us understanding and protect us from harm, both physical and spiritual.

Don't worry if your prayers don't include all these elements. Pray from your heart, and pray what you know is true of God from his Word. The apostle Paul said we ought to "never stop praying" (1 Thessalonians 5:17). That means, our prayer life should be an ongoing conversation with God that never ends.

Keep in mind that prayer is not a one-way phone call.

Listen for God's voice to speak to you. This may be with an impression placed on your heart, or it may be that the Spirit brings to your mind something from Scripture. Just take time to listen. Spend time in his presence, reflecting on his goodness and on his promises. And keep at it. God often uses our prayers to stretch our faith, so don't be surprised if the answers you seek don't come as quickly as you would like.

Fellowship

Now that you're a part of the family of God, you have many, many brothers and sisters! Christ followers come from every nation and every background, but they all share one thing in common: each and every one has been made new by Jesus.

The Bible says that from the earliest days of the church, believers "devoted themselves to the apostles' teaching and the fellowship, to the breaking of bread and the prayers" (Acts 2:42 ESV). This means that they did life together, studying the Word of God, reminding each other of the gospel, sharing their joys and sorrows, and lifting one another up in prayer and encouragement, no matter what came their way. Just as it should be in a natural family, our spiritual brothers and sisters are there to love us and spur us on.

The author of the book of Hebrews instructs us, "And let us not neglect our meeting together, as some people do, but encourage one another, especially now that the day of his return is drawing near" (Hebrews 10:25). We miss out on something crucial if we do not spend time together as a family.

If you do not currently have a church home, look for one that values the Bible as the Word of God and preaches the gospel clearly and faithfully. In addition, faithful churches lift high the name of Jesus, are devoted to prayer, and strive to display the love of God in every situation. Because every church is a collection of sinners saved by grace, no church is perfect. So don't look for perfection! Look instead for a church that strives to follow Jesus in everything it does.

The Bible compares the local church to the body of Jesus:

Yes, the body has many different parts, not just one part. If the foot says, "I am not a part of the body because I am not a hand," that does not make it any less a part of the body. And if the ear says, "I am not part of the body because I amnot an eye," would that make it any less a part of the body? If the whole body were an eye, how would you hear? Or if your whole body were an ear, how would you smell anything?

But our bodies have many parts, and God has put each part just where he wants it. (1 Corinthians 12:14–18)

Every believer is essential to the church. Each one has received certain gifts from the Holy Spirit for the benefit of all the other members of the body. That means that you need the local church, and the local church needs you. Even if you wonder whether a disability or impairment might keep you from serving effectively, know that you are essential to the work of God in the church. He has a plan for you and a place for you. Your inclusion is not optional.

With that in mind, there are circumstances and seasons that may keep some believers from attending weekly services. If you find yourself in such a situation, please know that it doesn't mean that all fellowship should be cut off or that your prayers and gifts cannot benefit your brothers and sisters. In fact, it's during the most trying seasons of life that we need one another all the more. Stay connected as well as you can and remain open to the love and encouragement of your spiritual family.

THE IMAGE OF GOD

The Bible tells us that in the beginning, God created people "in his own image" (Genesis 1:27). But what exactly does that mean? Theologians and philosophers have debated the subject for centuries, wondering if the image we bear has something to do with our capacity to reason, our hunger for God, or our free will. While each of those traits can and should be yielded to God's service, none of them are equal to the image of God in us.

The Value of Life

At the most basic level, being made in God's image means we were made to resemble God. Just as children often look like their parents, we were designed to "look" a lot like God. Now, of course, that doesn't mean that you've got God's eyes or his nose. God is Spirit, and as such, he is invisible (Colossians 1:15). So, when the Bible says we were created in God's image, it means we were designed to reflect his beauty, goodness, and truth.

Every human being is an image-bearer, regardless of age, ability, or capacity. As such, every life is sacred. God made this abundantly clear when he told Noah, "If anyone takes a human life, that person's life will also be taken by human hands. For God made human beings in his own image" (Genesis 9:6). Murder carries a heavy penalty precisely because every person is an image-bearer of God. To attack a person is to attack the God they were made to represent.

The Gospel and the Image of God

Back in the garden of Eden, when our first parents chose to trust the lie of the serpent rather than the goodness of God, they invited sin into this world. Sin's power twisted and distorted creation, including our ability to reflect our Creator. While the image of God within us remains unbroken, no one is able to perfectly or completely bear that image. No one represents God the way they should.

No one, that is, except Jesus Christ.

Jesus is "the visible image of the invisible God" (Colossians 1:15). The author of the book of Hebrews tells us, "The Son radiates God's own glory and expresses the very character of God" (Hebrews 1:3). In other words, Jesus is the exact image of God, the perfect picture of his goodness, beauty, and truth. If we want to know what God is like, all we need to do is look to Jesus.

One of Jesus' closest friends, the apostle John, put it this way: "No one has ever seen God, but the one and only Son, who is himself God and is in closest relationship with the Father, has made him known" (John 1:18 NIV). Jesus came to model what it looks like to bear God's image, but he also came to change us from the inside out so that we, too, can reflect the heart of our heavenly Father.

The New Testament tells us that everyone who trusts in Jesus and follows him will one day look just like him. "Just as we have borne the image of the man of dust, we shall also bear the image of the man of heaven" (1 Corinthians 15:49 ESV). Apart from Jesus, we look an awful lot like our father Adam, broken and twisted by sin, but God has made us new so that, little by little, we will become more like his Son. And when Jesus returns, we will be restored completely, able to bear the image of God perfectly, just like Jesus. That's the hope we have because of the cross and the empty tomb.

In the meantime, we are to walk in step with the Spirit of God, who is at work within us. When we do that, we bear good fruit, specifically "love, joy, peace, patience, kindness, goodness, faithfulness, gentleness, and self-control" (Galatians 5:22–23). Jesus displayed these nine traits perfectly in his life, and as we produce this same fruit in our own lives, we show the world around us who God is and what he is like—just as we were always meant to.

That All May See the Works of God

Look around. You'll quickly see that many things in this world are not as they should be. We can feel it in our bones. It comes as an ache in the deepest parts of our being. And yet even in the admission that things are not "as they should be," we recognize there is coming a day when all things will be made new and goodness restored. And so we wait eagerly, though we are not alone in this waiting. The Bible says "all creation has been groaning as in the pains of childbirth" in longing for that day (Romans 8:22).

At times, it's natural to wonder why God does not restore creation this minute, why he allows suffering and brokenness to persist. We might ask him in prayer, "Lord, what is your purpose in allowing this pain and this heartache?" Though God may not reveal the specific details to you about your particular place of suffering, we know he is always good (Psalm 100:5). We also have this promise from his Word: "God causes all things to work together for the good of those who love God and are called according to his purpose for them" (Romans 8:28).

As Joni learned in her own life, God sometimes permits what he hates to accomplish what he loves. We see a beautiful example of this truth in the pages of the Gospels. As Jesus and his disciples were walking through the streets of

Jerusalem one day, they came upon a man who was born blind, begging in the street. The disciples asked the Lord, "Why was this man born blind? Was it because of his own sins or his parents' sins?" (John 9:2).

Jesus' answer shattered their expectations. He said that God had allowed the man to be born blind so that God's works might be put on display for everyone to see (v. 3). Jesus loved the man and even healed him. This episode debunks the myth that disability is brought about because of personal sin, family sin, or a curse of some kind. Instead, it reveals the value and dignity this man had as an image-bearer of God. The Lord's desire was for him to be loved and cared for without any stigma because of his disability— to be welcomed into society and friendship with others.

The most powerful testimonies in history have come from people who endured hardships and suffering, and yet still proclaimed the goodness of God. They were able to do so because they learned to lean on the Lord every day, to trust him in all things, and to rest in his promises. They did as Psalm 34 suggests: they tasted for themselves and discovered that God is good (v. 8).

If you are living with a disability or experiencing suffering of some kind, know that you are not alone. Scripture says, "The LORD is close to the brokenhearted" (Psalm 34:18). He loves you and cares for you. Though it may be difficult to see at the moment, he has a purpose for your life and for your suffering. Lean into his promises and trust him day by day. As you experience his faithfulness, proclaim his goodness to everyone you meet, that they too might have reason to praise his name.

BIBLE READING PLANS

BIBLE READING PLANS TO GET YOU STARTED

The Bible says this about itself: "All Scripture is inspired by God and is useful to teach us what is true and to make us realize what is wrong in our lives. It corrects us when we are wrong and teaches us to do what is right" (2 Timothy 3:16). That means that every word is valuable and worth reading. However, when Bible reading is new it can be helpful to begin with a guide. Rather than starting at the beginning (Genesis 1:1) or jumping around, it may be worthwhile to spend focused time picking up the major themes of Scripture.

For that reason, we have provided three separate reading plans to get you started. The first is a four-week plan that will walk you through the life and ministry of Jesus. The second is a five-week plan that will give you a survey of the Old Testament. And the third is a two-week plan designed to help you navigate Acts through Revelation in the New Testament.

Don't get discouraged if you miss a day. Just pick up where you left off. Also, if something you read doesn't quite make sense, don't give up. Jot down your questions, pray about them, and if you have the opportunity, discuss them with your pastor or a mature Christian in your life. Oftentimes, it's the passages we struggle through that end up having the greatest impact on our spiritual lives.

With all that in mind, take up and read!

GETTING TO KNOW JESUS: A 28-DAY READING PLAN

DAY	TITLE	SCRIPTURE
1	Jesus' Birth and Dedication	Luke 2:1–38
2	The Child Jesus in the Temple	Luke 2:41–52
3	Jesus' Baptism	Matthew 3:13–17
4	Jesus' Temptation and Rejection in Nazareth	Luke 4:1–30
5	Jesus Calls His First Disciples	Luke 5:1–11; Matthew 9:9–13
6	Jesus' Healing Ministry	Mark 5
7	The Sermon on the Mount	Matthew 5–7
8	Jesus' Miracles	Matthew 14:13–33
9	Jesus and Nicodemus	John 3:1–21
10	Jesus, the Good Shepherd	John 10

DAY	TITLE	SCRIPTURE
11	Jesus Raises Lazarus	John 11
12	Parables of the Kingdom	Mark 4:1–34
13	The Good Samaritan	Luke 10:25–37
14	Lost and Found	Luke 15
15	Parables on Prayer	Luke 18:1–14
16	A Warning to Always Be Prepared	Matthew 25
17	Jesus Enters Jerusalem	Luke 19:28–48
18	The Last Supper	Matthew 26:17–35
19	Jesus Washes His Disciples' Feet	John 13:1–35
20	The Vine and the Branches	John 15:1–17
21	Jesus Is Arrested	Luke 22:39–62

DAY	TITLE	SCRIPTURE
22	Jesus' Trials	Luke 22:63–23:25
23	The Crucifixion of Jesus	Luke 23:26–56
24	The Resurrection of Jesus	John 20:1–18
25	Jesus Appears to His Disciples	Luke 24:13–49
26	Jesus Appears to Thomas	John 20:19–29
27	Jesus Restores Peter	John 21:1–19
28	The Great Commission and Jesus' Ascension	Matthew 28:16–20; Acts 1:1–11

A JOURNEY THROUGH THE OLD TESTAMENT: A 35-DAY READING PLAN

DAY	TITLE	SCRIPTURE
1	Creation	Genesis 1:1–2:25
2	The Entrance of Sin	Genesis 3:1–24
3	Noah and the Flood	Genesis 6:1–8:22
4	Abraham Follows God	Genesis 12:1–8; 17:1–22
5	Sodom and Gomorrah	Genesis 18:16–19:29
6	Isaac, the Son of Promise	Genesis 12:1–5; 18:1–15; 21:1–7
7	Abraham's Faith Is Tested	Genesis 22:1–19
8	Isaac Loves Rebekah	Genesis 24:1–67
9	Jacob and Esau	Genesis 25:19–34; 27:1–40
10	Jacob Wrestles and Reconciles	Genesis 32:22–33:20

DAY	TITLE	SCRIPTURE
11	Joseph Sold into Slavery	Genesis 37:1–36; 39:1–23
12	Joseph Lifted Up	Genesis 41:1–57
13	A Family Reunion	Genesis 42:1–38; 45:1–28
14	Moses Saved and Called	Exodus 2:1–3:22
15	Rescued from Egypt	Exodus 12:1–42; 13:17–14:31
16	The Israelites in the Wilderness	Exodus 15:22–17:16
17	The Ten Commandments	Exodus 20:1–21
18	Israel and the Golden Calf	Exodus 32:1–35
19	Joshua in Command	Joshua 1:1–18; 3:1–17
20	Taking the Promised Land	Joshua 8:1–35; 11:1–23
21	The Lord Is with Gideon	Judges 6:1–7:25

DAY	TITLE	SCRIPTURE
22	God Works through Sampson	Judges 13:1–25; 16:1–31
23	The Calling of Samuel	1 Samuel 1:1–28; 3:1–21
24	Israel Receives a King	1 Samuel 8:1–10:1
25	God Rejects Saul and Chooses David	1 Samuel 15:1–16:13
26	David and Goliath	1 Samuel 17:1–58
27	King David's Reign	2 Samuel 5:1–6:15; 7:1–17
28	Solomon and His Wisdom	1 Kings 3:1–28; 4:29–34
29	The Temple of the Lord	1 Kings 6:1–38; 8:1–66
30	The Prophet Elijah	1 Kings 17:1–18:45
31	The Exile of the Northern Kingdom	2 Kings 17:1–41
32	The Fall of Jerusalem	2 Kings 25:1–30

DAY	TITLE	SCRIPTURE
33	Daniel in Babylon	Daniel 1:1–21; 6:1–28; 12:1–4
34	The Return and a New Temple	Ezra 1:1–11; 6:1–22
35	The Walls of Jerusalem Rebuilt	Nehemiah 2:1–20; 6:1–19

A JOURNEY FROM ACTS TO REVELATION: A 14-DAY READING PLAN

DAY	TITLE	SCRIPTURE
1	Welcome, Holy Spirit	Acts 2:1–47
2	Stephen, the Church's First Martyr	Acts 6:8–8:1
3	Saul Meets Jesus	Acts 9:1–31
4	The First Gentile Believers	Acts 10:1–11:18
5	Paul, the Missionary	Acts 13:1–52; 16:1–40
6	Our Sin and God's Salvation	Romans 3:1–31; 8:1–39
7	The Way of Love	1 Corinthians 12:1–13:13
8	Life in the Spirit	Galatians 5:16–6:10
9	The Promise of Jesus' Return	1 Thessalonians 4:13–5:11
10	The Hall of Faith	Hebrews 11:1–40

DAY	TITLE	SCRIPTURE
11	Wisdom for the Christian	James 1:1–2:26
12	The Love of God	1 John 3:1–4:21
13	Worship in Heaven	Revelation 4:1–5:14
14	The Happiest of Endings	Revelation 21:1–22:21

Notes

Notes

Notes

Notes

Notes

Notes

Notes

Notes

Notes

Notes

Notes

Notes

ABOUT JONI & FRIENDS

Nearly one billion people around the world live with a disability. Many of these individuals and their families live in poverty, pain, and despair. We want to change this. Joni and Friends is committed to bringing the gospel and practical resources to people impacted by disability around the globe.

For the past forty years, it has been our mission to present the hope of the gospel to people affected by disability through programs and outreaches around the world. We energize the church, moving people from a lack of awareness to inclusion. Our goal is to see people of all abilities embraced and woven into the fabric of worship, fellowship, and outreach in the local church. We also train and mentor people with disabilities to exercise their gifts of leadership and service in their churches and communities.

Our Biblical Commission: "Go out quickly in the streets and alleys of the town and bring in the poor, the crippled, the blind and the lame. . . . Go out to the roads and country lanes and compel them to come in, so that my house will be full" (Luke 14:21–23 NIV).

Our Vision: A world where every person with a disability finds hope, dignity, and their place in the body of Christ.

Our Mission: To glorify God as we communicate the gospel and mobilize the global church to evangelize, disciple, and serve people living with disability.

OUR PROGRAMS

Wheels for the World provides the gift of mobility along with the hope of the Gospel to people affected by disability worldwide.

Family Retreats offer a haven for families impacted by disability. In a fully accessible camp environment, families are cared for, rejuvenated, and encouraged in Christ.

International Family Retreats partners with local churches to provide Christ-centered care and encouragement in an accessible camp environment for families impacted by disability in developing countries.

Cause 4 Life equips students for leadership in disability ministry. Through hands-on internships, students learn how to impact their churches and communities for Christ, advocating for justice and equality for all people impacted by disability.

Church Training Resources equips churches to create a disability-welcoming environment through specialized publications and disability ministry training.

The Christian Institute on Disability is the leading authority on disability-related issues from a biblical perspective, offering higher education, ministry training, and public policy that promotes a biblical understanding of life, human dignity, and the value of all individuals.

Joni and Friends Radio provides hope and encouragement through Joni Eareckson Tada's *Joni* and *Friends and Diamonds in the Dust* radio programs.

The Joni and Friends Ministry Podcast is a weekly program that answers real questions about disability and explores practical ways the church can include all people, regardless of ability.

JONI AND FRIENDS

PO Box 3333
Agoura Hills, CA 91376-3333

joniandfriends.org // (818) 707-5664
Fax: (818) 707-2391 // TTY: (818) 707-9707